Editorial Project Manager
Jamie Liu, M.A.

Editor-in-Chief
Sharon Coan, M.S. Ed.

Cover Designers
Lesley Palmer
Janet Chadwick

Imaging
Ralph Olmedo, Jr.

Production Manager
Phil Garcia

Publisher
Mary D. Smith, M.S. Ed.

Teacher Created Resources

School Fonts II

Traditional Printing and Cursive, plus Fun Fonts

Timesaving SOFTWARE TOOLS for Teachers

User's Guide

Teacher Created Resources

Teacher Created Resources, Inc.
6421 Industry Way
Westminster, CA 92683
www.teachercreated.com

©2003 Teacher Created Resources, Inc.
and Inspire Graphics

Reprinted, 2005

Made in U.S.A.

Table of Contents

Contacting Technical Support

If you encounter any problems or have questions, please call our Technical Support or Customer Service at 888-343-4335

E-mail: custserv@teachercreated.com

Installation

Macintosh Users

For OS 8 and OS 9

1. Insert the CD into your CD-ROM drive.
2. Double-click to open the Fonts folder on the CD.
3. Select all the fonts and copy them into the Fonts folder inside the System folder on your computer.
4. Restart your computer.

For OS X

To allow all users on a computer access to the fonts:

1. Log in to OS X with administrator privileges (you will be asked for a password).
2. Double click the hard drive icon.
3. Open the Library folder.
4. Open the Fonts folder.
5. Copy the files from the Fonts folder on the CD-ROM to the Fonts folder on your hard drive.
6. Restart your computer.

To allow specific users of a computer access to the fonts:

1. Log in to Max OS X with the username and password of the user who will have access to the fonts.
2. Go to that user's "Home" folder.
3. Open the Library folder.
4. Open the Fonts folder.
5. Copy the files from the Fonts folder on the CD-ROM to the Fonts folder on your hard drive.

6. Repeat the above steps for each user who will have access to the fonts.
7. Restart your computer.

Windows Users

To install in *Windows 95/98/ME/NT/2000/XP*, follow the steps below.

1. Insert the CD into your CD-ROM drive.
2. If your Auto Insert Notification is on, the "School Fonts" start-up screen will appear.
3. Follow the prompts on your screen to install.

To install in *Windows 3.x* or if the start-up screen does not appear automatically, complete the following steps.

1. Insert the CD into your CD-ROM drive.
2. Click Start, then click Run.
3. Type "d:\setup" (where "d" is the letter of your CD-ROM drive *) in the Open box, and click OK.
4. Follow the prompts on your screen to install.

* If you are not sure of the letter of your CD-ROM drive, go to Start, Run, and click Browse. Click the down arrow in the Look In box, and select your CD-ROM drive. Select Setup, click Open, then click OK. This will start the setup program.

Notes: The name of each font in this collection is preceded by the letters **"LD"** in your font list. LD stands for Lettering Delights, the company that created these fonts.

Set your font size to at least **"36"** for the best display of any of these fonts.

To make a continuous blank line when using the following fonts: Modern Print Line, Modern Printer Trainer, Modern Cursive Lined, and Modern Cursive Trainer, use the underline key while holding down the Shift key.

Ideas for Using the Fonts

All of the fonts in this collection can be used with standard application programs such as Microsoft Word and AppleWorks to build custom assignments and individual exercises. These fonts will save preparation time and enhance your presentations.

Here are some ideas for using these fonts in the classroom.

* Create handwriting worksheets for the whole alphabet or specific letters your students are having difficulty with, such as: b, d, p, s, g, and j.

* Create customized name printing worksheets.

* Create worksheets for practicing phonics or spelling words on training lines.

* Have students choose any of the fun fonts to type a short story or do journal writing. This will motivate students to be excited about writing.

* Use the fun fonts to make banners, signs, bulletin board displays, calendars, awards and certificates, cards, newsletters, and messages to send home. Save the time normally spent creating these by hand, and enjoy spectacular display that can be modified to use again and again!

Traditional Print (LD Traditional Print)

Traditional Print

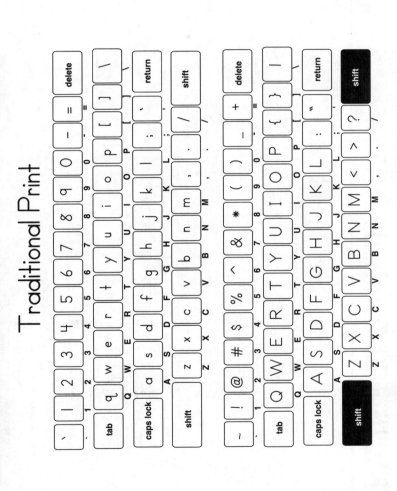

Traditional Print Lined (LD Traditional Print Lined)

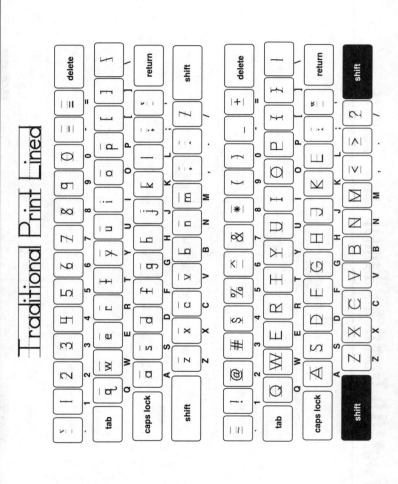

Traditional Print Lined

Traditional Print Trainer (LD Traditional Print Trainer)

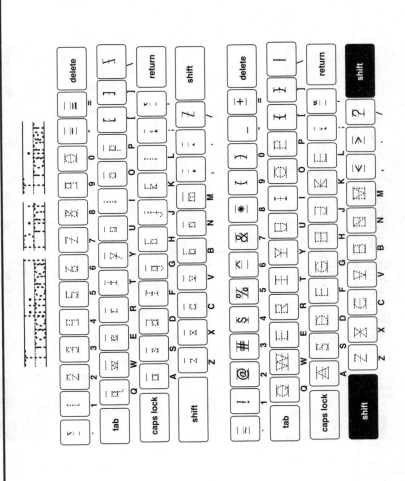

Traditional Cursive (LD Traditional Cursive)

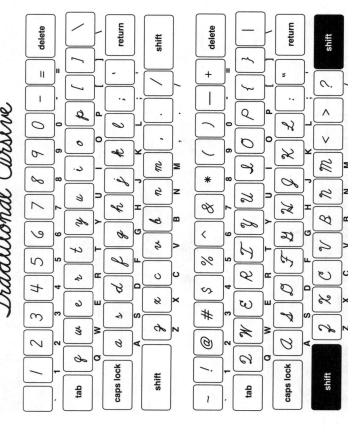

Traditional Cursive

Traditional Cursive Lined (LD Traditional Cursive Lined)

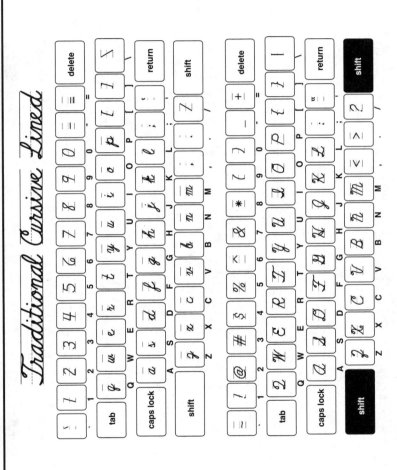

Traditional Cursive Trainer (LD Traditional Cursive Trainer)

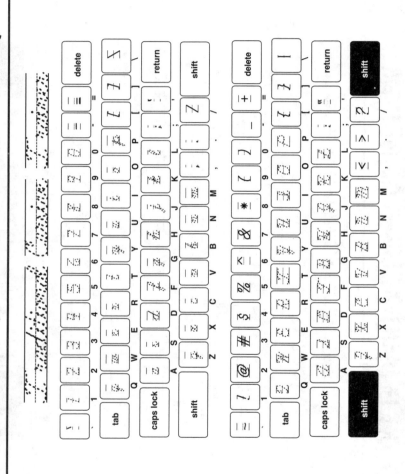

Circles (LD Circles)

Circles

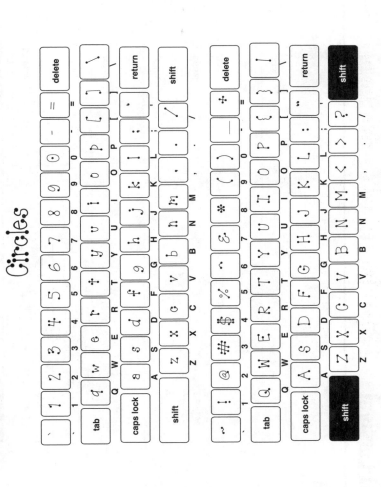

Cursive (LD Cursive)

Cute Curls (LD Cute Curls)

Cute Curls

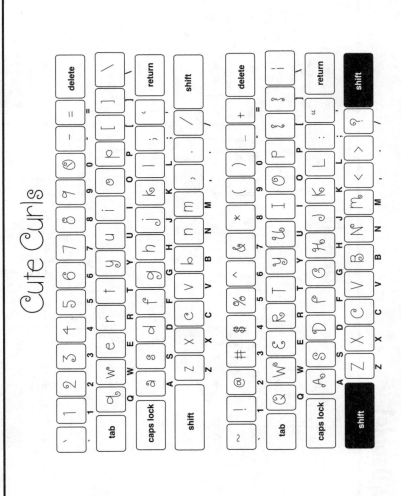

Dabble (LD Dabble)

Dabble

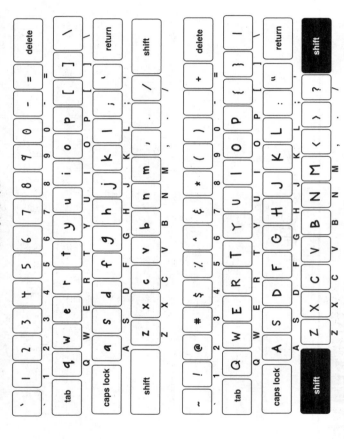

Elementary (LD Elementary)

Elementary

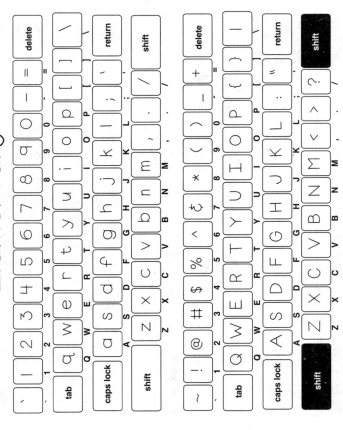

Falling Leaves (LD Falling Leaves)

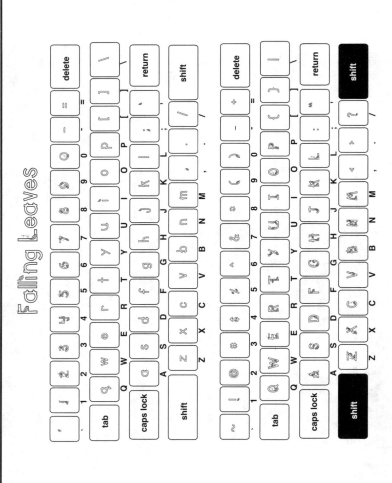

Flower (LD Flower)

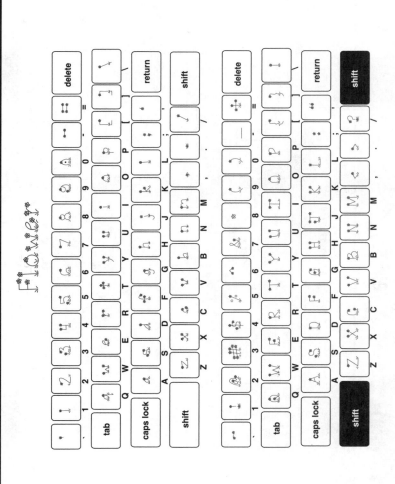

Formal

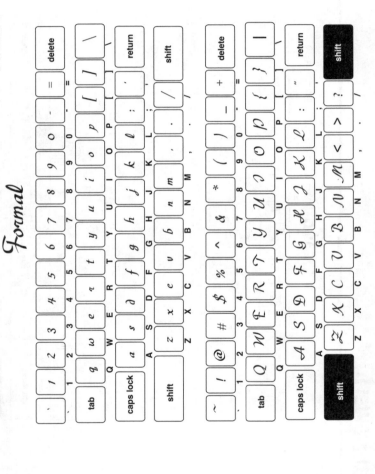

Scratchy Pen (LD Scratchy Pen)

Scratchy Pen

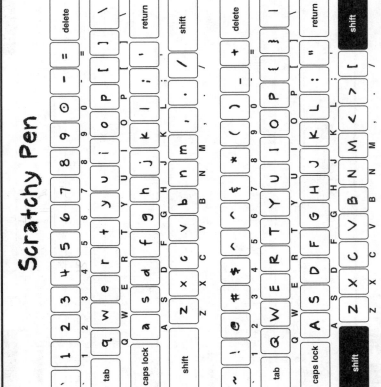

Sea Shells (LD Sea Shells)

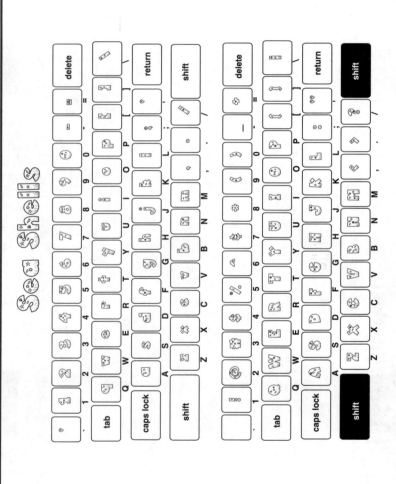

Shelly Print (LD Shelly Print)

Shelly Print

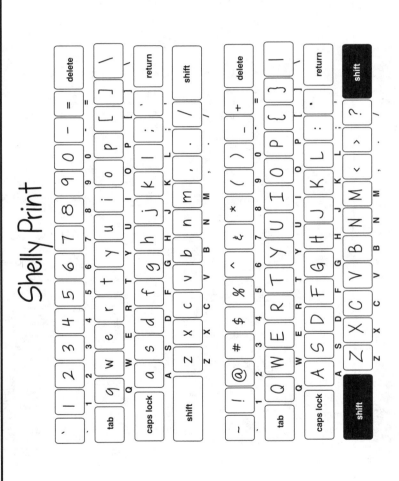

Simple (LD Simple)

Simple

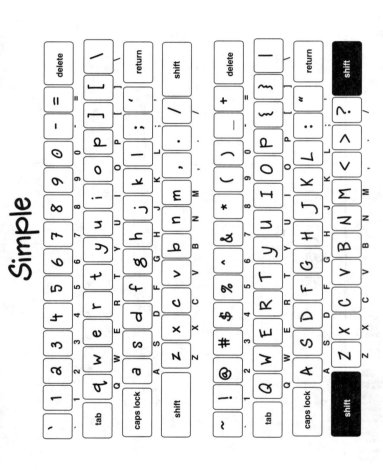

Snow (LD Snow)

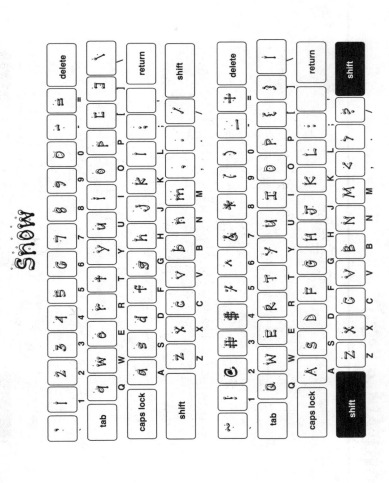

String Bean (LD String Bean)

String Bean

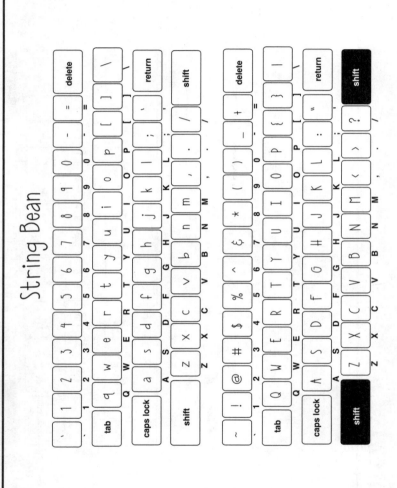